THE POWER OF THE "F" WORD IN THE WORKPLACE

WORKBOOK

5 Lessons

To increase your emotional intelligence

for effective workplace relationships

2nd Edition

AMANDA V. HILL

Lesson 1
How to identify my talents

LESSON 1

IDENTIFYING YOUR TALENTS

DISCUSSION 1.0

YOUR PASSION WILL ALIGN WITH WHAT YOUR NATURAL
TALENT IS.

WHAT COMES EASILY TO YOU?

LESSON 1

IDENTIFYING YOUR TALENTS

DISCUSSION 1.1

HOW YOU REACT TO PERSONAL LIFE EXPERIENCES IS
WHAT SHAPES YOUR CHARACTER?.

CAN YOU THINK OF A CHILDHOOD EXPERIENCE THAT HAS
SHAPED YOUR CHARACTER?

DISCUSSION 1.2

WHAT IF I TOLD PEOPLE IN THE COMPANY ABOUT MY FEELINGS TOWARDS SEEING MY WORK WITH MY SUPERVISOR'S NAME ON IT?

WHAT IF I DIDN'T FORGIVE HER AND SPOKE BADLY ABOUT HER TO OTHER SUPERVISORS BEFORE HER PASSING?

LESSON 1

IDENTIFYING YOUR TALENTS

PERSONAL REFLECTION

DISCUSSION 1.3

CAN YOU THINK OF SPECIFIC BEHAVIORS THAT IRRITATES YOU IN THE WORKPLACE?

TRY TO FOCUS ON THE BEHAVIOR, NOT THE PERSON. HOW DO YOU REACT TO THIS TYPE OF BEHAVIOR IN YOUR WORKPLACE?

CAN YOU THINK OF SOMEONE FROM YOUR PERSONAL LIFE THAT HAS THIS SAME BEHAVIOR?

EXAMPLE

LESSON 1

IDENTIFYING YOUR TALENTS

PERSONAL REFLECTION

DISCUSSION 1.3

HOW DO YOU INTERACT WITH THIS PERSON
WHEN THEY DEMONSTRATE THIS BEHAVIOR,
IN YOUR PERSONAL LIFE?

IS YOUR INTERACT SIMILAR TO HOW YOU
REACT TO THE PERSON IN THE WORKPLACE?

LESSON 1

IDENTIFYING YOUR TALENTS

PERSONAL REFLECTION

LESSON 1

IDENTIFYING YOUR TALENTS

PERSONAL REFLECTION

LESSON 1

DISCUSSION 1.4

CAN YOU THINK OF A PERSONAL LIFE CHANGING EVENT, WHERE YOU HAD TO CHOOSE TO PUSH THROUGH, AND NOT ALLOW IT TO STOP YOU FROM REACHING YOUR GOAL?

LESSON 1

IDENTIFYING YOUR TALENTS

PERSONAL REFLECTION

LESSON 1

DISCUSSION 1.5

WHAT KEEPS YOU UP AT NIGHT?

HOW DO YOU DEAL WITH STRESS? WOULD YOU CONSIDER IT HEALTHY?

WHAT IF I ASKED YOU TO DO THE BEST YOU CAN, WITH WHATEVER IT IS AND LET IT GO? HOW DOES THAT THOUGHT MAKE YOU FEEL?

FOR SOME PEOPLE THE IDEA OF "LETTING GO", THE THOUGHT ALONE BRINGS THEM STRESS. IS STRESSING OUT ABOUT A TASK HELPING YOU GET TO THE GOAL FASTER?

CAN YOU THINK OF ANOTHER WAY TO HANDLE A HIGH-PRESSURE SITUATION?

LESSON 1

IDENTIFYING YOUR TALENTS

PERSONAL REFLECTION

LESSON 1

IDENTIFYING YOUR TALENTS

PERSONAL REFLECTION

LESSON 1

IDENTIFYING YOUR TALENTS

PERSONAL REFLECTION

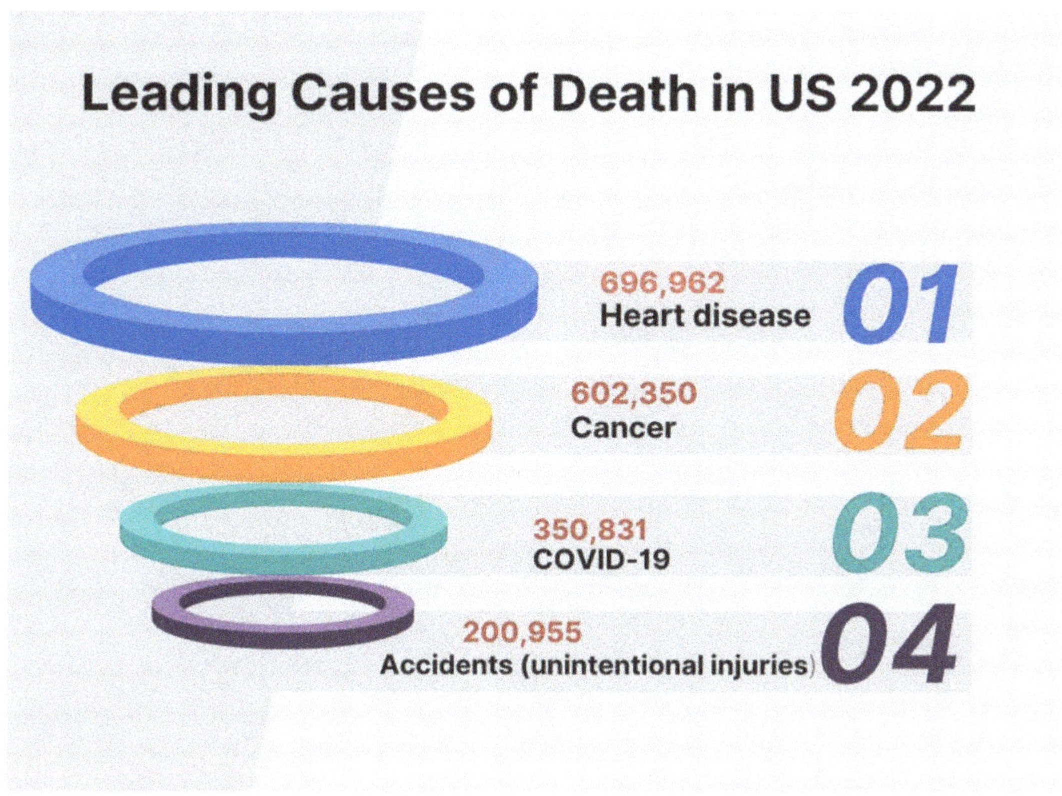

Statistics of Workplace Stress

80% of workers feel stress on the job, nearly half say they need help in learning how to manage stress and 42% say their coworkers need such help

25% have felt like screaming or shouting because of job stress, 10% are concerned about an individual at work they fear could become violent

14% of respondents had felt like striking a coworker in the past year, but didn't.

9% are aware of an assault or violent act in their workplace and 18% had experienced some sort of threat or verbal intimidation in the past year

Statistics of Workplace Stress

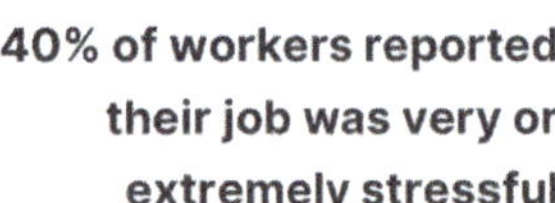

40% of workers reported their job was very or extremely stressful

25% view their jobs as the number one stressor in their lives

75% of employees believe that workers have more on-the-job stress than a generation ago

26% of workers said they were "often or very often burned out or stressed by their work

65% of workers said that workplace stress had caused difficulties and more than 10 percent described these as having major effects

10% said they work in an atmosphere where physical violence has occurred because of job stress and in this group

42% report that yelling and other verbal abuse is common

29% had yelled at co-workers because of workplace stress

14% said they work where machinery or equipment has been damaged because of workplace rage

LESSON 1

IDENTIFYING YOUR TALENTS

DISCUSSION 1.6

BASED OFF OF THE FEEDBACK ABOVE, 80% OF WORKERS FEEL STRESS ON THE JOB, NEARLY HALF SAY THEY NEED HELP IN LEARNING HOW TO MANAGE STRESS, AND 42% SAY THEIR COWORKERS NEED SUCH HELP.

HOW DO YOU HANDLE YOUR STRESS LEVEL AT WORK?

WHERE DOES YOUR STRESS LEVEL FALL ON A SCALE OF 1 TO 10?

LESSON 1

IDENTIFYING YOUR TALENTS

PERSONAL REFLECTION

LESSON 1

IDENTIFYING YOUR TALENTS

PERSONAL REFLECTION

LESSON 1

IDENTIFYING YOUR TALENTS

PERSONAL REFLECTION

Lesson 2

Uncomfortable

Use words to describe what it means to you when you feel uncomfortable:

____

____

____

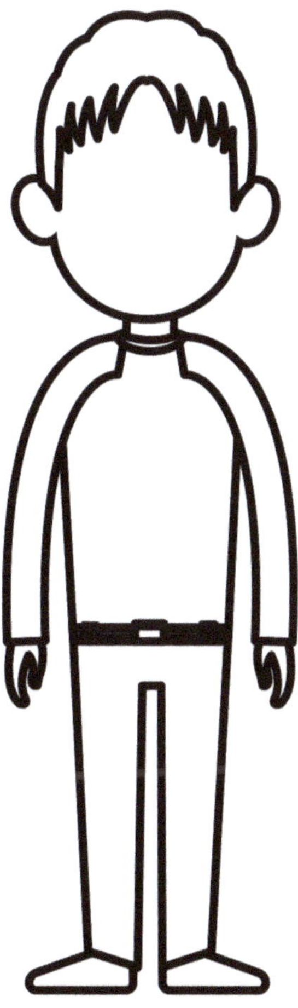

On the body, label the early waring signs your body gives off when feel uncomfortable or unsafe. Eg, tummy = butterflies.

LESSON 2

DISCUSSION 2.0

FROM A SCALE OF 1 TO 10, HOW EASILY ARE YOU DISTRACTED WITH LIFE EXPERIENCES, THAT IN TURN, AFFECTS YOU IN THE WORKPLACE? EXAMPLE

PERSONAL REFLECTION

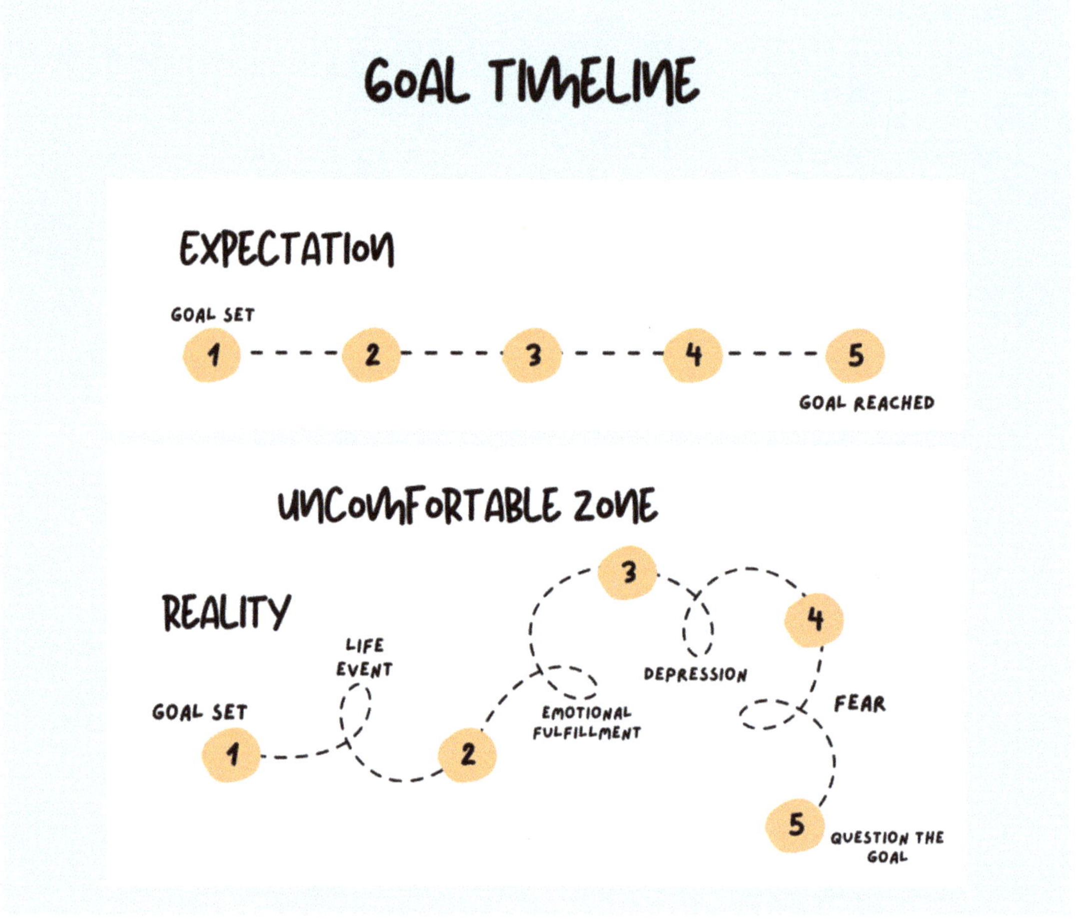

YOU ARE ONLY LIMITED TO THE LIMITATIONS OF YOUR OWN MIND

Amanda Hill

LESSON 2

GETTING USED TO BEING UNCOMFORTABLE

DISCUSSION 2.1

HAVE YOU EVER DREAMT OF SOMETHING BIG OR HAD A
PASSION FOR A DIFFERENT LIFESTYLE AND "LIFE" HAPPEN?

HOW DID YOU HANDLE THIS?

DID YOU CONTINUE TO PURSUE IT? EXAMPLE

LESSON 2
GETTING USED TO BEING UNCOMFORTABLE

PERSONAL REFLECTION

LESSON 2

GETTING USED TO BEING UNCOMFORTABLE

DISCUSSION 2.2

WHAT EMOTIONAL FULFILLMENT GIVES YOU YOUR "TEMPORARY FIX"?

CAN YOU THINK OF A HEALTHY WAY TO GET PASS STRESSFUL MOMENTS?

LESSON 2

GETTING USED TO BEING UNCOMFORTABLE

PERSONAL REFLECTION

LESSON 2

GETTING USED TO BEING UNCOMFORTABLE

PERSONAL REFLECTION

LESSON 2

GETTING USED TO BEING UNCOMFORTABLE

PERSONAL REFLECTION

Lesson 3

THE DISTANCE
BETWEEN
DREAM AND
REALITY IS
CALLED
DISCIPLINE.

DISCUSSION 3.0

LIST ONE AREA IN YOUR LIFE WHERE YOU NEED STRUCTURE.

WHAT RESULTS ARE YOU CURRENTLY GETTING IN THIS AREA?

DO YOU SEE A PATTERN OF BAD OUTCOMES IN THIS AREA?

LESSON 3

DO I NEED DISCIPLINE TO REACH MY GOAL

PERSONAL REFLECTION

LESSON 3

DISCUSSION 3.0

WHERE DO YOU NEED MORE FREEDOM IN YOUR LIFE?

WHERE YOU ADD MORE DISCIPLINE TO CREATE THOSE AREAS OF FREEDOM?

DO YOU CREATE HEALTHY BOUNDARIES IN YOUR LIFE TO ELIMINATE CONFUSION OR CHAOS IN YOUR LIFE?

WHEN YOU DO YOU NEED TO CREATE MORE HEALTHY BOUNDARIES?

LESSON 3

DO I NEED DISCIPLINE TO REACH MY GOAL

DISCUSSION 3.1

WHAT AREA OF YOUR CHILDHOOD DO YOU
FEEL WERE DYSFUNCTIONAL?

DO YOU SEE ANY PATTERNS IN YOUR
CURRENT LIFE THAT MIRRORS YOUR
CHILDHOOD EXPERIENCE?

DO YOU FIND IT HARD TO CREATE ORDER IN
YOUR CURRENT LIFE?

WHAT STEPS CAN YOU TAKE TO ADD ORDER
IN YOUR LIFE?

WHEN YOU THINK BACK TO YOUR CHILDHOOD
DO YOU SEE WHERE CHAOTIC BEHAVIOR WAS
DEMONSTRATED?

DO YOU TEND TO REACT IN THE WORKPLACE
IN A SIMILAR MATTER?

LESSON 3
DO I NEED DISCIPLINE TO REACH MY GOAL

PERSONAL REFLECTION

LESSON 3

DO I NEED DISCIPLINE TO REACH MY GOAL

PERSONAL REFLECTION

LESSON 3

DO I NEED DISCIPLINE TO REACH MY GOAL

PERSONAL REFLECTION

LESSON 4

MISTAKE & FORGIVE

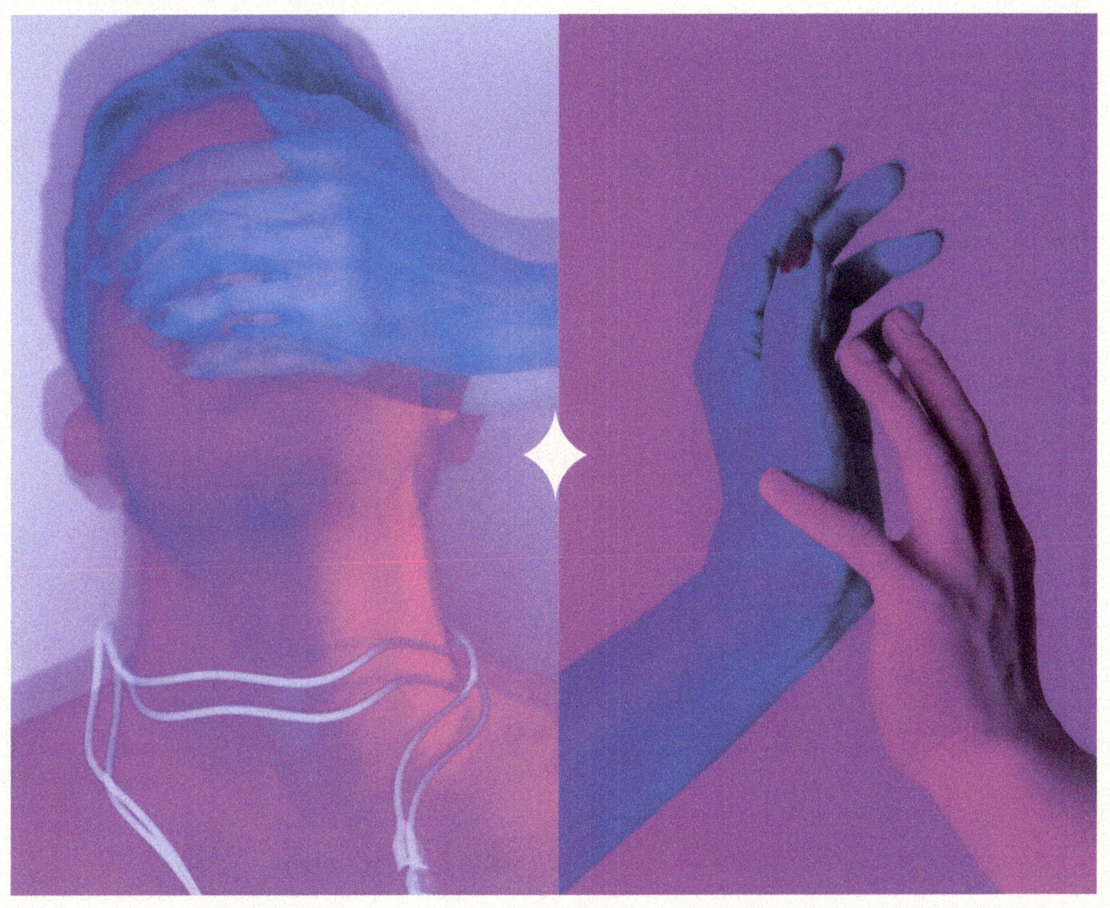

Forgiveness doesn't mean you are weak as a human, but by forgiving you are a strong person with a big heart.

LESSON 4

DISCUSSION 4.0

HOW CAN A LEADER ENSURE ANOTHER EMPLOYEE THAT THEY AREN'T HOLDING A GRUDGE?

LESSON 4

HOW DOES FORGIVENESS HELP ME IN THE WORKPLACE?

PERSONAL REFLECTION

LESSON 4

HOW DOES FORGIVENESS HELP ME IN THE WORKPLACE?

DISCUSSION 4.1

DO YOU HAVE ANY ILL FEELINGS TOWARDS A COWORKER? IF YES, HOW IS THIS AFFECTING YOU PHYSICALLY OR MENTALLY?

LESSON 4

HOW DOES FORGIVENESS HELP ME IN THE WORKPLACE?

PERSONAL REFLECTION

LESSON 4

HOW DOES FORGIVENESS HELP ME IN THE WORKPLACE?

PERSONAL REFLECTION

SELF *love*

IN THE SPACES BELOW, LIST ALL THE WAYS YOU CAN SHOW
LOVE AND APPRECIATION TO YOURSELF

LESSON 5

HOW DO I FORGIVE?

DISCUSSION 5.0

THINK OF A TIME WHERE SOMEONE DID NOT LET GO OF
SOMETHING YOU DID IN THE PAST. HOW DID IT MAKE
YOU FEEL?

ARE YOU REPEATING THIS BEHAVIOR TOWARDS
SOMEONE IN YOUR LIFE TODAY?

LESSON 5

HOW TO FORGIVE?

PERSONAL REFLECTION

DISCUSSION 5.0

CAN YOU MAKE A DECISION TO FORGIVE AND LET GO?

CAN YOU THINK OF A PERSON IN YOUR WORKPLACE THAT YOU NEED TO FORGIVE? CAN YOU LOOK AT THE INNOCENT?

ARE YOU WILLING TO LET IT GO, AND OPEN UP NEW OPPORTUNITIES IN YOUR FUTURE?

LESSON 5
HOW TO FORGIVE

PERSONAL REFLECTION

LESSON 5

HOW TO FORGIVE

PERSONAL REFLECTION

LESSON 5

HOW TO FORGIVE?

PERSONAL REFLECTION

PERSONAL REFLECTION

FORGIVE

Forgiveness
is
for you,
not for them.

LESSON 5

HOW TO FORGIVE?

PERSONAL REFLECTION

FORGIVENESS ACTION
plan

GOAL	START DATE:	DUE DATE:

PROGRESS: 0% ☐☐☐☐☐☐☐☐☐☐☐ 100%

ACTION STEPS

POSSIBLE OBSTACLES

HOW TO OVERCOME OBSTACLES

FORGIVENESS ACTION *plan*

GOAL	START DATE:	DUE DATE:

PROGRESS:　　　0%　☐☐☐☐☐☐☐☐☐☐　100%

ACTION STEPS

POSSIBLE OBSTACLES

HOW TO OVERCOME OBSTACLES

FORGIVENESS ACTION
plan

GOAL	START DATE:	DUE DATE:

PROGRESS: 0% ☐☐☐☐☐☐☐☐☐☐ 100%

ACTION STEPS

POSSIBLE OBSTACLES

HOW TO OVERCOME OBSTACLES

FORGIVENESS ACTION
plan

GOAL	START DATE:	DUE DATE:

PROGRESS: 0%   [ ][ ][ ][ ][ ][ ][ ][ ][ ][ ]   100%

ACTION STEPS

POSSIBLE OBSTACLES

HOW TO OVERCOME OBSTACLES

FORGIVENESS ACTION *plan*

GOAL	START DATE:	DUE DATE:

PROGRESS: 0%   100%

ACTION STEPS

POSSIBLE OBSTACLES

HOW TO OVERCOME OBSTACLES

www.ingramcontent.com/pod-product-compliance
Lightning Source LLC
Chambersburg PA
CBHW041816110726
48006CB00019B/2399